Anecdotes from a Nihilist

Matthew Leonard

BookLeaf
Publishing

India | USA | UK

Presentation by *BookLeaf Publishing*

Web: www.bookleafpub.com

E-mail: info@bookleafpub.com

ISBN: 9789358319286

First edition 2024

A Martyr for the Sake of Cause

A martyr for the sake of cause
Undefinable for the sake of logic
Always wanting to put on pause
Something eternally tragic
And that be my damnation
Striving for something romantic
But ending up acting frantic
It was just a front
A facade put up by ego
And hoping that she
Would never go
To the land of milk and honey
Ever in search of needed opportunity
To make amends
With a bad romance
Yet she is caught
In an endless dance
That is
Capitalism
A love for the sake of commodity
And a commodity produced for the sake of God

Note from an Anarchist

Institutions seek to civilize us
Yet they only demonize us
Give us false credence
And put us against each other
Yet we should stand together
And fight this godless nihilist power
It's just like the tower
In Babylon
That collapses
As the world goes on
And we all speak different languages
And our train tracks
Are on different gauges
It's like freedom is being held hostage
Waiting for us to pay homage
To the namesake of freedom
But not the concept
Yet the underlying precept
Is essentially illegalist doctrine
Made legal
By a hegemony
That lies beyond us

Common Good

The common good
Is never as it should
Only if something would
Prompt change
Bring about reform
Cause a true storm
In the midst of the people
Yet most are like sheeple
Unable to think for themselves
And lacking agency
Isn't that giving credence
To the ignorant
Rather than the dissident
Who will cause incident
In the house of reason
Which is ever-pervaded with dogma
I guess we'll need a revolution
To figure that one out

On the Path

Every day
You gotta pray
For that pay
And for that yay
A grade
An evaluation
A misfortune
At opportunities mischaracterized
It is only something everlasting
That has superficiality
And only something temporary
That is deep
Yet you should
Keep your head
And get out of bed
And get back to work
As there's an eternal
Fork in the road
Between discipline
And being showed
That you are not the man you think you are
Only the potential
Of what you could be
Godspeed

Martyr without Suffering

In the grind
You will find
That it is mind over matter
And should instead of rather
And work instead of banter
Isn't that mischaracterized
As an obsession
Or a contradiction
That you should be disciplined
Instead of christened
About being a martyr without suffering
Or a man without substance
But nothing will keep you
From that grievance
That you failed
To put in the work that you should
Instead of thinking of excuses that could
And you start looking for your own good
Ain't that smooth

Your Friend, Strife

Sometimes you put everything to a cause
Yet you should put everything on pause
To reflect about your devotion
And something causing endless commotion
In your soul
For we worship a God outside of us
Yet can't reconcile what's inside of us
With that reality ever biting
All you ever think about is fighting
Yet there isn't a haven in heaven
Or the devil in love
Or a mistake in brethren
Or an orgy of doves
Yet there are mistakes in life
And a root to Strife
You just need to stop
Looking at the damn knife
For your cause
Without reason and without pause
Is devotion to the hard end
Rather than the knife
And you seek in a friend
Everlasting console
That you can do something
To ease your soul

But nothing ever works
It's just a notebook of ideas
And a lot of lulls
About a life mislived
Or a knife misplaced
Or something measles
That you can't get right
Or something that bites
Your very essence
You blame it all on adolescence
Yet you felt nothing in the presence
Of God almighty
Maker of heaven and Earth
And the lord prays dearly
That you'll make a rebirth
To a common good
And bountiful food
And that all things fall into place
As they should
And that endless race
That is life
Puts an end to your friend
Everlasting strife

Martyr by Faith

Nihilist by circumstance
Martyr by faith
Everything is torment
I am becoming a wraith
Gods wrath
Or the wrath of man
Cannot stop
The brilliance that is math
For it is my craft
Above all else
Structure reigns supreme
Math is my God
It eases my pain
And I worship it dearly
For it brings me sanctity
Mas-allah
And all that is infinite
Can be brought to finitude
A comprehension
An understanding
Structure withstanding
A conjecture demanding
Patience and discipline above all else
I am forgetting myself
Just let that sublime ideal go away

And let reality stay
For it will never betray
That faith in structure

And all Young Men Dream of the Spring

Why can't I escape the past
I was trying to go fast
But put myself last
And am left with a sort of amnesia
Those feelings just escaped in the breeze, yah
I had wanted to forget
All my regret
I would always fret
About the path I am on
And my past is all gone
Only bitterness in my mouth
And thoughts in my head
Might I one day return
To my old homestead
And all my concern
Go away with the sunset
I was looking for the perfect bet
Something to gamble my life away
And twice I failed at that very adage
And all young men dream of the spring
Of new memories and everlasting love
Of wild escapedes and moments
When push comes to shove
And to dreams of youth

Which would burn ever brilliantly
On the backdrop of their potential
Spring is the time of rebirth
When we harness our gifts of the Earth
And chastise feeling
Without keeling
To a dream gone by
And a dream realized
Finally something has materialized
And that one day
You'll have something you can call
Your own

Karma

Karma eventually hits empires
Who act on capitalistic desires
Karma is a force of nature
And a God to man
There is no resistance
You can only stand
In the face of your punishment
Or your reward
It just depends
If you were steward
To something moral
Or something ethical
Yet neither hold true
In the cause of misfortune
Karma seeks to transform you
Into a better person
Without reservation
Karma is the force of the universe
Dictated by frequency
Causing delinquency
Among those
Who know misfortune
All they do
Is attract more of it
And create a situation

Utterly intolerable
And that is their curse

Searching for a Lullaby

Every man yearns for something
Anything really
Like a drug to distract
An act to detract
A person to attack
Something to ease their pain
To shut off their mind
To do something kind
To themselves
Something easy
Like stocking shelves
Yet distraction is only temporary
And you are left
With your own thoughts
And left
To your own device
And that is your vice
That you have liberty
But are shackled
To something you do not know
But it is always there
And you always hear
Life's so unfair
It isn't
God just did things

To make you stronger
Against the wit
Of your own

Elegant but Wrong

Something can be elegant, but wrong
Graceful, but strong
Isolated, but among
People
It is like your running
Up a steep hill
Yet it is all worthless
Unless you out a worth to it
Like art
Put out
By a peddler
Hoping to make a dime
Hoping in time
Someone will find worth
In his work
Just as he has
Found
Something of which
He can rebound
Like a stray bullet
Hitting armor
A thing like that
Is art in the right eyes
It just takes the taste of an artist
To bring out that experience

And that artist
Gives credence to the avant garde
Just as the guard
Remains steadfast to his post
An ode to duty
And an ode to himself

A Mathematician's Ode to Society

Every mathematician
Looks for contradiction
In argument
In proof
Yet they remain aloof
To the logic of society
And it's inherent flaws
In that you get paid
Without having anything made
Except symbols on paper
You aren't no waiter
Instead you conjure up ideas
That may have use
In 100 years
If even
And even then
You just produce
More symbols
To describe an engine
Or describe a car
Something like that
Can go very far
Yet you see no use in the present
Only symbols on paper

And you think
"Every mathematician's a bourgeois decadent"

Every Scientist was an Anarchist

In every free man
There is something dying to be let out
Something holding him slave
To a version of him he could be
Like a tree enslaved by concrete
But something forces him to let it out
In such a way it becomes perverse
And nothing can reverse
That
Yet this is merely a shift
In the thing dying to be let out
Something pure and innocent
That has been distorted and shackled
By unnatural constraints
And to be something
Organic
Yet artificial
A combination of the two
Gives birth to something new
And every scientist
Was an anarchist and a fascist
At the same time
And anarchy
Breeds innovation

For the sole purpose to survive
To understand this
Means to thrive

Illusion, Delusion, or Repression

Everything is either illusion,
Delusion, or Repression
Yet the truth exists
To be suppressed
For you know it has power
And the people
Who just keep on giving
A nation
Of educated proletariat
Making products
To support the hegemony
Yet the Marxists are no better
Hypocritical
To a point
That their truth
Has to be suppressed
By delusions
That they are a grand moral power
And that they
Bring order to the world

Left to Fate

Some things are left to Fate
And some things take shape
In a new form
With new energy
Like a breath of fresh air
In a room
That's been stagnant
For over 300 years
It represents something new
Which makes us stronger
And changes our perspective
And brings more meaning
To our lives
This is something we should seek
Inside of us
And outside of us
A change in perspective
That could lead to a breakthrough
And something new
Which could follow through
These are the aspects of life
You should seek to live by

Demonstrations of Character

True demonstrations of character
Are only found in times of desperation
And nothing you do
Can serve as reparation
To the actions you do
And getting what others
Give to you
And what you give
Will come back to you
It could be something somber
Everlasting recollections
About a life
Filled with opportunities
And filled with strife
You won't find one
Without the other
And nothing you do
Can ever bother
The endless tides of the universe
Let this be to you
A lesson in karma

Certain torment

Certain torment
Never ends
And certain people
Are not your friends
And certain things
Are never disclosed
And certain houses
Are never foreclosed
No matter how behind
They are in payment
They need certain things to fail
And certain things to stray
So that they can continue
To receive pay
From a system made for them
And one without them
Would be radically different
I guess that is the dream
Of every anarchist
To live in a world
Where he can be free without Christ
And live
Without fear of repression
Of their views,
Their faith,

And their life

Left to Time

Things that are left to time
Eventually level out
And things that are left to time
Eventually reveal their answers
And situations
Which you thought were catastrophic
Turned out to be blessings
And all your Sufferinf
Turned you into a martyr
To worship God
And not let your suffering
Define you
It is all a true display of character
About what you can do
And how to do it
And eventually
The hours will overflow
Into results
That make you
Fat and happy

It ain't all free

Some day you'll see
It ain't all free
Some things must be
A lost job
A lost woman
An opportunity
For a different life
Yet nothing compares
To the freedom
To choose
To live
To manifest
Ideas
Yet conjured
And attract
Something jeweled
Like an austere day
In the mountains
Or tossing some coins
In a fountain
To make a wish
For a better life
One that
Deviates you from
Your radical tendencies

Condemnation

Eternal damnation
Is condemnation
Of behaviors
In a previous life
Of which
You caused much strife
Yet the cure
To this curse
Is through hard work
Some things could be worse
Like being falsely imprisoned
Falsely accused
Of crimes you didn't commit
Or something
That you really regret
And you'll fret
About your chance
To do it again
You are always a fan
Of illegalist doctrine
And propaganda by the deed
We live in an exploitative system
You should take heed
On how to capitalize yourself
At the expense of others

Some things change your mind

Some things are meant to stay
And others remain purely play
Some things stay the same
While others make you lane
Some things change your mind
And some things you'll never find
Some things change rapidly
And others stay the same happily
No matter your circumstance
Or the things prescribed to you
You will always
Have something new
To say
To do
It all just takes time
To find out
What god has done
For you

9 789358 319286